A Time Line to Old John

by

D.A. Ramsey

**V·O·L·C·A·N·O
PUBLISHING**

Volcano Publishing,
13 Little Lunnon,
Dunton Bassett,
Leicestershire,
LE17 5JR

© D.A. Ramsey 1996

Typeset in 11 pt Times

This booklet is sold subject to the condition
that it shall not, by way of trade or otherwise, be lent,
re-sold, hired out, or otherwise circulated without
the publishers' prior consent.

All rights reserved. No part of this publication may be
reproduced or transmitted in any form or by any means,
electronic or mechanical, including photography, recording
or any information retrieval system, without permission in writing
from the publishers.

ISBN 1 898884 05 6

Acknowledgements

First and foremost, my sincere thanks to Mrs. E. Bissill, Staffordshire, for allowing me access to her private archive concerning the management of the former Bradgate Estate and other Leicestershire papers.

To Mr. J. Scott-Bolton, FRICS for his patience in dealing with my enquiries, and all members of staff at the Leicestershire Records Office who have produced so many documents for me over the past twenty years. Few English records offices have escaped my attention and the chance discovery of interesting papers lodged at Chester, Northampton and Stratford-upon-Avon records offices concerning Bradgate villages is entirely due to these offices having easily understood filing systems

Tony Squires drew my attention to many details within papers, maps and other source material such as photographs, as well as providing useful comments as my research progressed.

John Hodgson, National Trust Archivist at the John Rylands Research Institute, University of Manchester for drawing my attention to many interesting items in the Dunham Massey Papers and for producing an excellent catalogue of the papers.

Mr. R. Burrows who has many times drawn my attention to the many alterations made by man in the fields surrounding Bradgate. As a practising farmer whose eye daily observes the subtle changes which occur in the land surface, the routeways, clay pits and brick kiln sites used when manufacturing bricks for Bradgate House were soon pinpointed.

Lastly to my wife Gloria, a sincere thank you for proof reading and correcting text and photograph captions.

Contents

Introduction .... (i)

A Time Line 1

Map of Bradgate Park 22/23

Old John 24

Mills on Bradgate Estate 29

The Tower and Horse Racing 35

Mow Cop and Old John 46

Introduction to the Bradgate Series of Books

This book is **Book 1** one of series of five books which collectively will answer some of the most frequently asked questions about *Bradgate* and its environs.

The starting point is a timeline from **1066 to 1976** which embraces local as well as national happenings, detailing how these events affected the management of a considerable estate, which by the mid 19th century had grown to some 11,645 acres in north-west Leicestershire. The myths and legends attached to **Old John** – that most famous of Leicestershire landmarks – are dealt with and some surprising and hitherto unknown facts are furnished for the very first time.

Readers will be surprised to find that 200 years ago potential Derby winning racehorses were brought together at *Bradgate* and raced in a series of time trials to assess their performance. Once a horse's capabilities were deemed of some merit, it would be spirited away and into Staffordshire for training – where it was less public – until the day of the race.

Book 2 deals with the staffing, food and drink at **Bradgate House** during the period 1678-1681. Excursions to markets as far away as Cambridge for the main shopping in bulk show how visiting a supermarket is certainly not a recent activity. Here is revealed a way of housekeeping at Bradgate House which remained almost unchanged from Tudor times c.1500 to 1681.

A complete schedule of stock held in the house was made on June 27th 1681. This records the wines, beers and foodstuffs held in the kitchen and cellars on that particular day and is probably the only published listing of its type available for a large 17th century house in Leicestershire.

Book 3 centres around a map of Bradgate which, by means of its marking was drawn in **1746** but its recorded features give detail to much earlier times, such as a vacated *Bradgate House*, outbuildings

Introduction

and routeways long since abandoned. In particular the location of the former 'village' or scattered settlement once known as 'Broadgate' can be ascertained with accuracy and the story behind the demise of the village can now be told.

Book 4 is another reference work in its own right and for anyone with county connections and an interest in family history, it is possible that hitherto unknown ancestors and their occupations will emerge from its pages. The villages around *Bradgate* have for centuries been the homes of families with familiar Leicestershire surnames and one surname in particular is connected with **Groby** for a continuous period of some seven hundred years! There are many surprises, possibly the biggest is that **Kirby Castle**, built by Lord Hastings between 1480 and 1484 took the bulk of its labour force from the villages belonging to the then Marquis of Dorset, Lord Grey of Groby.

The village of **Newtown Linford** is traced from its foundation in the 13th century, to the cutting down of **Charnwood Forest** and the tenants' wood-dealing activities in the 18th and 19th centuries. in **Book 5**. In here the war years of 1939-1946 are covered through the recollections of the late Fred Foulds who was the owner of the *Park View* café at the time. The slate quarrying activities in Swithland Woods and at Grey Lodge, Groby which also formed part of the Bradgate estate of the Earls of Stamford are also covered with an accuracy which indicates just when an individual or group was quarrying and in which hole in the ground they were to be found. A visit to **Swithland Woods** or **Bradgate** will never be the same.

All five books in the series are based on primary source material which has been collected over a period of some twenty years by the author. Each is illustrated by original maps and diagrams together with photographs, some old whilst others of more recent origin.

A TIME LINE
Events concerning the Bradgate Estate in chronological order.

1066	Hugh de Grentlemaisnell held six carucates of Groby land. Petronilla his daughter married Robert Blanchmains, Earl of Leicester. By marriage the Manor of Groby passed to Robert de Quincey, Earl of Winton and from him to William Ferrers*, 2nd son of the Earl of Derby who was created Baron Groby.
1086	In Groby 6 carucates of land less 3 bovate. Land for four ploughs. In Lordship 2. Ten villagers with One Freeman and Five smallholders have 3 ploughs. Woodland 2 leagues long and ½ league wide to the value was 20s; now 60s.
1086	In Ratby 6c. of land less 3 b. Land for 6 ploughs. In Lordship Two ploughs, with One slave. Ten villagers with a priest and Five smallholders have Four ploughs. A mill at 28d. The value was 20s; now 60s. 2c. of land of the jurisdiction of these are in 'Bromkinsthorpe'; 3 in Desford; ½ in Glenfield; ½ in Braunstone.
1086	In Anstey 2c. of land. Land for four ploughs. In Lordship One; Four slaves. 13 villagers with 4 smallholders have 2 ploughs. Meadow, 8 acres; woodland 2 furlongs long and One furlong wide. The value was 10s; now 40s.
1088	Labouring population: Bradgate villages:- Source VCH Leicestershire:

Anstey	21
Bradgate	0
Cropston	0
Glenfield	12
Groby	16
Kirby Muxloe	8
Newtown Linford	0
Newtown Unthank	0
Ratby	17
Thurcaston	30
Whittington	0

1134	Ulverscroft Priory founded by Robert Bossu 2nd Earl of Leicester.
1216	Henry III crowned.

A time line...Events

1241	Bradgate Park first mentioned "the rights to take deer with nine bows and six hounds" given to Roger de Quincey, Earl of Winchester, by Hugh d'Albini, Earl of Arundel and Lord of Barrow.
1247	The above rights re-granted to Roger de Quincey by Roger de Somery, Lord of Barrow and successor to Hugh d' Albini.
1272	Henry III dies, his son Edward I in Palestine at the time of death.
1274	Edward I crowned at Westminster.
1279*	William de Ferrers inherits Bradgate and Groby Estates.
1280	Itinerary: Newtown Linford, Rothley; Swithland, Anstey, Bradgate and Cropston answered collectively as one village.
1286	William Ferrers held manor and wood in Charnwood.
1287	Custody of Groby and Bradgate estates given to to Nicholas Seagrave until Ferrers heir came of age.
1288	Groby Park established by this date.
1293	Newtown Linford first mention of rent paying tenants.
1302	William Roceby held Manor.
1305	William Ferrers, for Ulverscroft Priory held 67 acres of waste.
1307	Edward I dies of dysentery near Carlisle, July 7th.
1307	Edward II proclaimed king at Carlisle.
1316	William Ferrers now has possession of the Manor.
1327	Edward II dies September 20th.
1327	Edward III crowned.
1338	Henry Ferrers has grant to hold market in Groby.
1342	A grievous distemper raged in Leicester, of which numbers died. It was attended with such violent pains, that the cries of the afflicted were like the yelling of a dog. (Thoresby: *History of Leicester*).
1343	Henry de Ferrers, grandson of William dies.
1343	Isabella, wife of Henry holds one third of the manor of Groby with a quarry of slates in Groby and Swithland.
1345	Thomas de Ferrers leaves land and advowson of Bunney, Nottinghamshire, to prior and convent of Ulverscroft.
1348/49	Initial attack of the Black Death of Northern Europe – The Great Plague of Edward III. 50,000 die in London and grass grew in the streets of Bristol. It is believed that 2,000 die in Leicester – or a third of the population. This causes scarcity of labour and higher wages.

A time line...Events

1361/62 Epidemic in England – Leicester 1361.
1369 Epidemic – Renewal of Anglo-French war.
1370 William de Ferrers dies; his wife Margaret holds one third of the Manor and the whole of Bradgate Park.
1371 Cal Close Rolls 'the whole of Bradgate Park as enclosed by walls, ditches, hays and palings – one whole enclosure called the Shetehedges – the whole of Blakenhay as enclosed – a third of Ladies Hay – a third part of Stewards Hay towards the east.
1375 Epidemic.
1377 July: Coronation of Richard II.
1377 Poll Tax – Bradgate Villages – source VCH Volume III

Anstey	88	
Bradgate	41 total only 29 pay (MVN)	
Cropston	54	
Groby	75	receipts 66
Markfield	62 paid	
Newtown Linford	62	
Ratby	85 paid	
Swithland	62	
Thurcaston	85	

1381 Great Revolt or Peasants' Revolt. Main centres of disorder in Kent Essex, East Anglia, Cambridgeshire, Hertfordshire, Buckinghamshire, Cheshire, Leicestershire, Northamptonshire, Somerset, Warwickshire and Yorkshire.
1389 Truce with France.
1390 Epidemic
1396 Twenty-eight year truce with France.
1399 Richard II deposed.
1399 Henry IV (first of the Lancastrian kings).
1400 First record of beer (made with hops) being imported: it came in through Winchelsea and was not for sale, but for Dutch merchants working in England.
1405 Epidemic
1413 Epidemic
1413 Henry IV dies from an epileptic fit 20th March 1413.
1413 Henry V crowned in April.

A time line...Events

1422	Henry V dies at Vincennes near Paris.
1422	Henry VI only nine months old comes to throne.
1424	Bond: Roger Holand, and Thomas Holand his son, both of Newtown Lynforth lease le Shotehedges Wood, Groby.
1428	First record of hops being successfully grown in England.
1433	Epidemic.
1434	Epidemic.
1437	Epidemic.
1438/9	Food shortages after bad harvest.
1439	Epidemic.
1444	Epidemic.
1444/5	Bond: Roger Holand, and Thomas Holand his son, both of Newtown Lynforth lease Shotehedges for wood and underwood.
1445	William de Ferrers dies and IPM shows one third of the arable of the Manor worth nothing because it lay fallow.
1445	The Grey family inherit the Manor of Groby and Bradgate Park.
1446	Sir Edward Grey becomes Lord Ferrers of Groby. He obtains a special dispensation from the Archbishop of Canterbury to have his expected child christened in the manor house chapel at Groby.
1448/50	Epidemics
1452	Epidemic
1454	Sir Thomas Grey of Astley, Warwickshire, becomes Earl of Huntingdon.
1457	Elizabeth Woodville marries Sir John Grey.
1460	Sir John Grey dies – killed at the second battle of St. Albans.
1461	Sir Thomas Grey succeeds as Lord Ferrers of Groby.
1461	Edward IV proclaimed king (first Yorkist king). The Greys lose their estates.
1464	Epidemic.
1464	Edward IV marries Elizabeth Woodville secretly at Grafton Regis, Northamptonshire. Greys' estates returned.
1465	Elizabeth Woodville crowned Queen at Westminster. Soon afterwards arrangements are made for:- Elizabeth's father to become 1st Earl Rivers. Elizabeth's brother to become Lord Scales by marriage.

A time line...Events

1465   Elizabeth's son from her first marriage to Sir Thomas Grey to become Earl of Huntingdon, later still he becomes 1st Marquis of Dorset. He marries Cicely Bonneville, grand-daughter and heiress of the exiled Duke of Exeter. Later, Elizabeth's daughter Elizabeth of York, becomes the wife of Henry VII.
Edward IV and Elizabeth also had two sons, Edward V and Richard Duke of York; both murdered in 1483.
The Astley estates near Nuneaton, are returned to the Grey family and the 1st Marquis of Dorset and his wife reside there.

1465   Leicestershire Priories of Ulverscroft and Charley united.
1471   Epidemic.
1471   Lord Ferrers of Groby becomes Earl of Huntingdon.
1475   Thomas, Earl of Huntingdon becomes Marquis of Dorset.
1479   Epidemic.
1480   Kirby Castle building begins using red brick.
1483   Edward V, not yet thirteen accedes. On the way to London from Ludlow Castle the Duke of Gloucester intercepts group and arrests Earl Rivers and Lord Grey. Edward is removed from the group and taken to the Tower until his coronation.
1483   Duke of Gloucester declared Protector of the Realm.
1483   Earl Grey executed in Pontefract Castle on the orders of Richard Duke of Gloucester.
1483   Thomas Grey 1st Marquis of Dorset flees to the continent.
1483   Richard III declared king 26th June 1483.
1484   Kirby Castle building stops following the beheading of Lord Hastings.
1485   Epidemic.
1485   Battle of Bosworth. Richard III slain. Henry VII accedes.
1485   Thomas Grey returns to England and regains most of the former estate but not Groby Park.
1491   John Beron, John Turvyll and Robert Fouleshurst, clerk release to Robert Fouleshurst, knight all their lands in Groby.
1492   Elizabeth Woodville imprisoned in a monastery at Bermondsey dies.
1492   Christopher Columbus sails to the West Indies and 'discovers' cocoa. pineapples and turkeys – examples of which are brought back to England.

A time line...Events

1493	Epidemic
1494	Robert Fouleshurst, knight grants to Ralph Shirley, knight, Hugh Eggerton, Thomas Kebull (of Humberstone – Sergeant at Law), William Ashby, Thomas Entwesell, Master Richard Eggerton, clerk and Master Robert Fouleshurst his Manor of Glenfield also tenements and rents at Groby and Syston.
1496	Land exchange concerning Bradgate between Thomas Grey and Abbot of Garendon.
1497	Grant in Tailmale to Thomas Marquis of Dorset "all those messuages, cottages, stables, houses, building, gardens and lands in Calais, between in called 'Pryncess Inne' on the south and tenements of John Mulshoe and John Priket on the north, Sewerstreet on the east and Frerestreet on the west.
1498?	Thomas Grey builds two towers in brick at Groby, Old Hall, the second tower is not completed when building starts at Bradgate.
1499	Land exchange between Abbot of Garendon, Prior of Ulverscroft and Marquis allows enlargement of original park at Bradgate.
1499	Epidemic.
1500	The building of Bradgate House is started using red brick (clamp fired) in Dumples Field close by.
1500	Epidemic.
1500	First pocket watch made in Germany.
1501	Thomas Grey, 1st Marquis of Dorset dies.
1505	Epidemic.
1507	Thomas Grey, 2nd Marquis of Dorset imprisoned in Calais and the Tower of London by Henry VII.
1509	2nd Marquis released as Henry VII dies of consumption.
1509	Henry VIII accedes to the throne of England.
1512	Groby Park returned to Thomas Grey, 2nd Marquis of Dorset.
1512	William Skevyngton Bradgate Park keeper.
1517	Plague very active in Leicestershire.
1519	Plague very active in Leicester.
1519	Thomas, 2nd Marquis of Dorset, grants lease of 99 years to Abbot of Garendon in lieu of like lease from him for like term, of all their lands, tenements, reversions and services at Bradgate, except a yearly rent paid by him to the Prior of Ulverscroft.

A time line...Events

1519	In Causeway Lane, Cropston a hamlet of houses known by the name 'Broadgate' is pulled down. The tenants of 'Broadgate' are re-housed in Newtown Linford Parish towards Markfield. The new settlement is also called 'Cottagers Close' – the same name as that given to the enclosure, alongside the 'Broadgate' from which they had just moved.
1520	February 6th, 2nd Marquis of Dorset appears in Chancery to answer charges of enclosure by his late father and the prior of Ulverscroft and the Abbot of Garendon.
1521	Epidemic – plague very active in Leicestershire.
1524	Thomas Grey becomes Chief Justice of all the King's Forests, dies at Astley near Nuneaton.
1526	Plague very active in Leicestershire.
1530	Henry Grey succeeds as 3rd Marquis of Dorset.
1530	Wolsey arrested on charge of high treason. He dies at Leicester Abbey whilst being taken to London.
1530	There are at least 825 religious houses in England and Wales: 502 monasteries, 136 nunneries and 187 friaries containing 7,500 men and 1,800 women, or one in every 375 of the population.
1535	*Valour Ecclesiasticus* – The Royal Commissioners' Valuation of monasteries, nunneries and friaries reveals that the total income of all these religious houses is somewhere in the region of £160,000 to £200,000 per annum, or three quarters as much again as the average crown income at the same date.
1536	Dissolution of the Smaller Monasteries; (about 350 dissolved including Garendon near Loughborough).
1537	Lady Jane Grey born.
1537	The Manor of Loughborough passes to the Grey family.
1539	Dissolution of Larger Monasteries (about 250 dissolved).
1539N	Ulverscroft surrendered to the King by the Prior Edward Dalby and seven canons: Thomas Wymondeswold, Richard Eglate, William Smythe, Thomas Mason, William Betton – cellarer, William Bland and George Smythe. (Thomas Massey sub-prior).

A time line...Events

1540	Observations by Leland travelling from Bradgate to Groby. "A mile and a half much by wooded land. Newer works and buildings there (Groby Hall) by the Lord Thomas 1st Marquis of Dorset among which works he began and erected the foundation and walls of a great gate house of brick, and a tower, but that was left half unfinished by and so it standeth yet".
1540	Kitebridge, near Sheethedges Wood, Groby held by Richard Elison.
1540	Stewards Hey held by John Somersfield.
1540	Sheethedges and le Nether Pole held by John Colbrande.
1540	March 8th Thomas Manners, Earl of Rutland given manors of Garendon and Swithland among others.
1540	Lord Grey involved with treasonable act. Loses Beaumanor to the Crown.
1541	Easter term: Margaret, widow of 2nd Marquis of Dorset summoned to answer for the enclosures made by the Abbot of Garendon at Bradgate.
1543	Plague very active in Leicestershire.
1543	The Priory of Ulverscroft and adjoining lands granted to Thomas, first Earl of Rutland who sells to Sir Andrew Judd, Lord Mayor of London.
1547	January 28th, Henry VIII dies of a slow disease. He leaves Edward, son of Jane Seymour, Mary, daughter of Katherine of Aragon and Elizabeth, daughter of Anne Boleyn.
1547	Henry Grey, Marquis of Dorset, made Constable of England.
1547	Edward VI crowned at Westminster – he is only ten years old and in poor health.
1550	Ulverscroft Priory and Charley sold to Henry, Marquis of Dorset.
1550	Henry Grey, Marquis of Dorset, made Justice of the King's Forest.
1551	Deflation: 50% devaluation of coinage. Effects: rise in prices, fall in value of sterling abroad.
1551	Sweating sickness reported in Darley Dale, Derbyshire.
1551	Henry Grey, Marquis of Dorset created Duke of Suffolk.
1552	Lord Guildford Dudley, son of the Earl of Northumberland, marries Lady Jane Grey. Northumberland senior knows that he will lose power if Mary should come to the throne.
1553	Edward V1 dies of consumption July 6th.

A time line...Events

1553   Lady Jane Grey proclaimed Queen of England by Earl of Northumberland.

1553   Grey estates including Bradgate taken by the crown. Groby and Beaumanor retained by Frances, Duchess of Suffolk.

1554   Lady Jane Grey and her father Henry Grey beheaded 24.02.1554.

1554   Most of Loughborough Manor passes to Sir Edward Hastings but not Beaumanor, this stays with Frances, Duchess of Suffolk.

1554   On the death of Henry Grey Ulverscroft and Charley granted to Frideswide Strelly by Queen Mary.

1554   Suffolk followers Leonard Dannett, gent, Thomas Dannett, gent, George Medley, esquire, Bartholomew Wullocke, gent, and John Boyer pardoned.

1554   The Duchess of Suffolk, Lady Jane's mother remarries Adrian Stokes and together they live at Beaumanor.

1556   Poor Laws. Provision for those who could not work. Those who would not work were to be compelled to. Tobacco first introduced into England.

1556   Parliament ordains that all men who keep more than 120 sheep should keep one cow per sixty sheep and rear one calf per 120 sheep.

1557/58   Plague very active in Leicestershire.

1558   Death of Mary I. Elizabeth I proclaimed Queen.

1558*   Calais lost in war against French this was the last continental possession of England.

1558/9   Influenza epidemic in Leicestershire.

1559/61   Plague active in Leicester - St Martin parish register.

1564   First house at Wigston to record a chamber, or upper room within a house. (W.G. Hoskins – *The Midland Peasant*).

1564   Victims of the plague kept off the streets of Leicester.

A time line...Events

1564	Number of families living in:
	Anstey 24
	Botcheston 5
	Bradgate 27 (Bradgate House, Park staff, keepers, grooms etc)
	Cropston 14
	Groby 21
	Newtown Linford 47 (in Groby Manor - excluding Bradgate)
	Ratby 27
	Stanton u Bardon 14
	Swithland 30
	Thurcaston 25
1565	John Wilson, nephew of Frideswide Strelly becomes owner of Ulverscroft and Charley on the death of his aunt.
1565	First pencil made in Switzerland. It is made with graphite enclosed by a wooden cover.
1569/72	Groby woodland referred to as Le Morthowe = The dead alders, and Le Shaw 'Martinshaw wood' is derived from the combination of these names – Morthoweshaw = Martinshaw.
1572/75	Woodland held by Henry Skypewith
1575	Groby Manor, Bradgate Park and fields eastwards towards Cropston returned to the Greys.
1578	Ambrose Wilson, son of John Wilson becomes the owner of Ulverscroft and Charley.
1578	30th May: John Grey sells Enville to Henry Grey of Groby and Beckbury to his cousin John Haughton
1579	Henry Grey buys Manor of Ratby.
1582	Plague year in London - 30 deaths in St Martin's parish Leicester.
1583	Glazed windows first recorded at Wigston. John Browne, Yeoman. (W.G. Hoskins - The Midland Peasant)
1585	Tobacco and potatoes introduced into England by Sir Walter Raleigh after his visit to America. Potatoes are not immediately embraced as a food crop in England. Writers first observe fields of potatoes being grown in Leicestershire in the 1680s. The Irish realise the potato's value from very shortly after their introduction from the Americas.
1586	Plague in Derby and Chesterfield.

A time line...Events

1587   Mary Queen of Scots executed.
1587   Henry Grey knighted.
1588   Philip II of Spain launches an 'Invincible Armada' against England – it is destroyed by the English naval fleet and severe storms around the British Isles.
1589   Legislation on Cottages. No cottage should be built for a land labourer unless it possessed 4 acres of land. (Legislation repealed in 1775)
1592/3   Plague in Derby.
1593/4   Plague active in Leicester.
1595   Spaniards land in Cornwall – they burn Mousehole and Penzance.
1601   Poor Law: Parishes to raise money for the poor, Alms houses set up for the old, hospitals for the sick. Refusal to work is made a punishable offence.
1603   Elizabeth I dies March 24th.
1603   Pestilence in Leicester.
1603   Sir Henry Grey of Pirgo, an only son, made Baron Grey of Groby. He moves to Bradgate.
1603   James I crowned King of England & Scotland, July 25th.
1605   Plague in Ashbourne, Derbyshire.
1607   Plague in Leicester.
1608/9   Plague in Chesterfield, Derbyshire.
1609   Ulverscroft Priory and 1358 acres of land sold to Robert Peshall by Ambrose Wilson. By the marriage of Peshall's daughter it passes to Sir Robert Bosseville.
1610/11   Plague very active in Leicester.
Leicester watchmen are armed with crossbows and bolts. "So they may shewte att the plague visited persons as would not be kept in their houses!"
1611   Plague very active in Loughborough.
1611   Plague very active in Loughborough.
1613   Manor of Ratby restored to Greys. Previously seized by king.
1614   Henry, Baron Grey of Groby dies – Henry Grey his grandson who was to become the first Earl of Stamford succeeds.

A time line...Events

1615 Plague very active in Leicester.
1616 Australia discovered by Dirck Hartog a Dutchman.
1620 John Grey marries Anne Cecil daughter and co-heiress of Cecil family. Anne bore five daughters and four sons.
1623 Plague very active in Leicestershire 13/14 years.
1625 James I dies of a tertian ague on March 27th.
1625 Contagious sickness in the town of Ashby. 15 persons die over a period of three months, the plague is thought to account for 9 of these.
1625 Charles I becomes king.
1625/26 Plague very active in Leicester.
1628 Henry Grey created 1st Earl of Stamford 26th March. In early life he resided at Bradgate 'where his haughty, irritable disposition made him unpleasant.'
1631 Loughborough visited by the plague 135 die.
1635 Charles 1st - an affirmation by Charles of Queen Elizabeth's original grant in 1574 - Groby Manor -Bradgate Park and lands. 16.05.1635.
1636 Plague in Derby - small outbreak in Leicester.
1636 11th May - on nomination of William Earl of Exeter, Samuel Bordman and Randle Cotgrave receive Groby Manor to administer. 1th May.1636.
1636 Groby Manor alienated to William Earl of Exeter – Henry Grey's wife's father!
1637 Plague in Derby.
1638/39 Plague in Leicester again widespread - pest houses again brought into use 17 houses affected - dead total 41.
1640 A letter sent between London and Edinburgh now takes ten days.
1641 Plague raged in several towns and villages in the neighbourhood of Leicester, Market Harborough, Birstall, Thurmaston and Whetstone.
1642 Outbreak of Civil War on August 22nd.
1642 The first stairs recorded in Wigston. Robert Brabson, Yeoman, Permanent stairs remain very rare, not only in Wigston but elsewhere before 1650 (W.G.Hoskins - *Midland Peasant*).

A time line...Events

1643 Excise duty put on soap. Duties remain until 1853.
1648 Plague again in Leicester.
1649 Charles the 1st beheaded January 30th.
1649 The Commonwealth and rise of Cromwell.
1650c Mansell designs the first beer glass, a type of cylindrical beaker which was large and heavy. Glasses of this type are purchased for Bradgate House in 1679.
1651 Import duty on sugar introduced. Best quality sugar = 16s 1d coarsest sugar = 1s 5d (see 1846 for repeal of this tax)
1657 Thomas, Lord Grey of Groby dies.
1658 Oliver Cromwell dies.
1660 Restoration of monarchy - Charles II.
1662 Hearth Tax levied at 2/- per hearth and this tax lasted until 1689, Tax collected by parish constable.
1665/66 Plague very active Eyam, Derbyshire between September 1665 and October 1666.
1667 Burial in wool, Legislation in 1667, more strictly enforced after 1678, Acts repealed in 1814.
1670 Hearth Tax returns indicate the following number of households:

Anstey	66
Bradgate	1
Glenfield	35
Groby	59 (29 paying & 33 exempt) (sic)
Newtown Linford	48
Markfield	68
Ratby	55 (29 paying & 26 exempt)
Swithland	42
Thurcaston	36

1673 Henry Grey 1st Earl of Stamford dies - buried in private chapel vault Bradgate.
1673 Thomas Grey becomes 2nd Earl of Stamford.
1676 Ecclesiastical population census:

Anstey	140	Cropston	53
Glenfield	101	Markfield	143
Swithland	138	Thurcaston	91

A time line...Events

1679	Abraham Bunney, a farmer of Ratby paid 5/- for playing his viol at Bradgate on ye 12th day after Christmas.
1679	12 Beer glasses purchased at 6 pence each for Bradgate House. (See 1650 entry .)
1683	An attempt on the life of Charles II leads to Bradgate House being searched for arms.
1685	Thomas Grey joins the Duke of Monmouth's Rebellion, Thomas arrested and sent to the Tower on treason charge, later pardoned.
1685	Charles II dies of apoplexy leaving no lawful children.
1685	James succeeds his brother Charles to become James II.
1688	Rebellion which brings change of fortune to Grey family and Privy Council Post for Thomas Grey.
1689	Hearth Tax ends.
1689	William III and Mary II rule.
1694	William III rules alone.
1696	Window tax replacing Hearth tax imposed by parliament - lasts in various forms until 1851.
1696	William III visits Bradgate and improvements are made to House, stables and approach roads in readiness for the visit.
1702	The 2nd Earl's marriage to Mary, daughter of John Oldbury, a London merchant brings a fortune of £40,000 as a dowry but little contentment to the Earl for 'they quarrelled and lived in the same house as absolute strangers to each other bed and board,'
1702	William III dies after a fall from his horse.
1702	Queen Anne becomes queen.
1714	George I becomes king.
1716	Thomas Grey, 2nd Earl of Stamford dies without an heir.
1716	Harry Grey, cousin of Thomas, becomes 3rd Earl of Stamford.
1719	Freeholders: ten in Groby parish.
1720	Dunham Massey House, stables and Booth mansion in Chester rebuilt.
1727	George I dies.
1727	George II succeeds.
1730/40	Families in Thurcaston = 87

A time line...Events

1736	Henry Grey, the future 4th Earl of Stamford, marries Lady Mary Booth and thereafter Dunham Massey becomes one of the Greys three principal seats. Enville Hall, Staffs. and Bradgate, Leics. being the other two.
1736	The Earl of Stamford's Estate rents: Leicestershire rents and profits £1968 18s 2d Staffordshire rents and profits £1654 15s 2d Derby/Notts rents and profits £1544 12s
1739	Henry Grey dies his son Henry becomes 4th Earl of Stamford. Enville Hall becomes the principal house.
1739	John Carter, estate Steward, has garden walls to Bradgate house repaired and gateways bricked up. This encloses 22 acres of grassland.
1739	Paid Mr Herrick, John Needham and John Spencer for 36 sheep to be put in Bradgate Park. £14. 2s.6d. For having them brought to Bradgate 1/-.
1739*	Bradgate House would now appear to be in ruins or abandoned.
1740	Bradgate Park wall building on west and north perimeters begins.
1746	The Glass Excise Act introduced which puts a tax on glass goods by weight. This leads to the introduction of lighter bottles and, more elegant and highly decorated drinking glasses.
1748N	November 7th: There is a terrible fire at Thurcaston, with several houses, barns, stables and hay ricks, household furniture and implements of husbandry, consumed to the ground. (p1057 Vol III pt 11 Nichols).
1751	Heavy tax imposed on gin.
1760	George II dies of heart attack.
1760	George III becomes king.
1760	Bradgate Estate steward Joseph Hooley allows rent and wood sales arrears to reach £4, 259 8s 9d.
1761	Anstey enclosure.
1762	Leicestershire Est rents and profits £3743 8s 1d
1762	Staffordshire Est rents and profits £1639 14s 9d
1762	Derby/Notts Est rents and profits £1564 14s 3d

A time line...Events

1767N	From May to December, 27 persons die of a malignant fever in the town of Anstey. (Nichols p1057 Vol III pt II)
1768	Henry Grey, 4th Earl dies. George – Harry Grey becomes 5th Earl Of Stamford.
1768	Henry Hind (Junior) takes lease of Groby slate quarry near the Ashby Road. Seemingly a holding lease to prevent others developing the site. Small amount of slate extracted 1768-1770.
1770	Ratby enclosure.
1775	Freeholders: Fifteen in Groby Parish (the same total as 1716)
1781	New stable for eleven horses built in Bradgate.
1781	Cropston enclosure.
1782	Earl of Stamford gives blankets to his distressed neighbours in the area of Stewards Hey, Groby. This is seen as excellent charity and is long remembered.
1784	'The Earl of Stamford has given to the poor in the neighbourhood of Stewards Hay, 40 guineas which he has directed to be laid out in procuring for them such necessaries as bread, coals, linen for shirts, sheets etc.' Newspaper report in Leicester Journal.
1784	Racehorse tax starts. A tax on the possessions of racehorses from 1784 to 1874.
1784	Windmill on John Hill and water mill (also within park and close to Bradgate House) stop working, Windmill removed and water mill decays.
1784	Autumn: the tower on John Hill - now known as Old John Tower - built by Sketchley an Anstey mason and builder.
1784	Windmill erected on Lent Hill Newtown Linford.
1786	Earl of Stamford's son George - Harry, future 6th Earl of Stamford comes of age. The celebrations include a large bonfire on John Hill.
1787	Groby school built.
1787	Bradgate Dovecot roof, mill and men's rooms repaired by Sketchley.
1789	Groby enclosure.
1792	Walling on the east and west of Bradgate Park perimeters begins.
1796	The 5th Earl of Stamford becomes Baron Delamare and Earl of Warrington in addition to his first title.

A time line...Events

1800c	Lent Hill mill stops working and Ulverscroft mill takes over the task of grinding the Newtown grain.
1800	Parliamentary return shows Groby as 60 families 163 males, 136 females in all 299. Of these 168 employed in agriculture.
1801	First official population census 9 million in England and Wales.
1801	Population counts: Groby 299, Newtown Linford 377, Ratby 480
1814/15	Blakes Hay Farm, Newtown renovated, slates from Mr Hind, Swithland.
1818	Lent Hill Farm, Newtown, known also as 'The Buck's Head' (alehouse) rebuilt by Benjamin Rudkin, Newtown builder - slates from Swithland slate works of William Johnson.
1819	George - Harry 5th Earl of Stamford dies and his son George - Harry becomes 6th Earl of Stamford.
1821	Holgates Hill plantation (24 acres) begun. Walling by Swinfield.
1822	Newtown Linford Sunday School built for £86 1s 5d.
1822	New cow shed built in the Dumples Field, Bradgate.
1822	Number of deer in Bradgate Park = 299.
1823	Thomas Frith builds wall on Charnwood Forest fences.
1823	Number of deer in Bradgate Park = 263.
1825	Thomas Frith builds walls around plantations at Brockercliffe, The Oaks & Blakehay Farm.
1827	William Chaplin, the Earl's gamekeeper at Groby, shot and wounded whilst on patrol in Whittington Rough, near Markfield. His dog is killed by poachers. Chaplin recovers. John Upton is found guilty and sentenced to be transported for seven years. John Sutton and William Ball fined £50.00 plus probationary period. Thomas Dilkes gives King's Evidence.
1828	Thomas Frith builds walls around new plantations at Sharpley Hill and Benscliffe, Newtown.
1829	On the death of Mrs Bosseville the Rev. A. Emerson became the owner of Ulverscroft Priory.
1830	George III dies leaving no children.
1830	William IV, George III's brother succeeds.
1830	June - Flooding in Bradgate Meadows causes three feet of water to enter the house of Head Park Keeper, Henry Adams.

A time line...Events

1831   Thomas Frith builds new wall around John Hill plantation (2 acres).
1831   Parties visiting Bradgate are numerous and not acting with correct decency and decorum. William Martin (Land Agent) inserts advertisement in Leicester Journal to deter those indulging in such objectionable excesses.
1831   Both George and Robert Stephenson visit Groby and assess the possibility of railway between village and Leicester and Swannington line.
1831   Newtown Linford contains 74 houses – 549 inhabitants in parish. Rev Curtis.
1832   Groby Granite Railway linking the Leicester and Swannington line with Groby opens.
1833   A new slate quarry opens at Groby leased by Parsons and Gill.
1833   (May) – Parsons has already thirty men employed in the new slate works at Groby.
1833   Thomas Chaplin's new dairy, cellar and cheese room built at Groby.
1833   After many years of neglect the Earl of Stamford begins renovation of Newtown Linford houses and building of new cottages there.
1833   Bradgate: Dimmingsdale (or Hare Spinney) begun (4 acres)
1833   Five fish weirs built by Rudkin in BradgatePark.
1833   Granite from village quarry in Groby to Marylebone, via canal, to meet 5,000 ton order.
1833   November. Robert Stephenson visits Groby to look over proposed extension of Groby railway to slate works.
1833   November:
Granite is taken from Groby village to West Bridge via railway then barges from there to London destinations.
Prices for delivery at:-
Brentford   13/3d per ton
Paddington   13/6d per ton – rough form,
Marylebone   11/3d per ton.
1834   Bradgate Park: Bowling Green Hill Plantation, (13 acres) walled by Frith and planted by Stokes.
1836   Bradgate Park: Deer Barn Plantation, (6 acres) & Groby Copy or Coppice Plantation (15 acres) begun.
1836   Number of deer in Bradgate Park = 297

A time line...Events

1837 William IV dies.
1837 Newtown Linford church enlarged.
1837 Victoria becomes Queen at 18.
1837 Bradgate: Thorn (2 acres) and Holly Plantations walled by Frith and planted by Stokes.
1837 Copt Oak school built.
1837 Number of deer in Bradgate Park = 332.
1838 Number of deer in Bradgate Park = 359.
1840 Groby church built for £2,260. Only £122 12s comes from public subscription the Earl pays the balance.
1840 Copy Plantation walling begins.
1841 Bradgate: Planting of Copy Plantation begins.
1841 Groby – twenty-nine estate cottages at this time.
1841 Newtown Linford: thirteen estate cottages at this time.
1842 Groby: New school built for £250 3s 9d.
1843 Groby: thirty-three estate cottages at this time.
1843 Newtown Linford: thirteen estate cottages at this time.
1845 George – Harry 6th Earl of Stamford dies his grandson, also George – Harry becomes the 7th Earl of Stamford at the age of eighteen. He inherits three huge estates in Leicestershire, Cheshire and Staffordshire and a rent roll of £90,000 per year.
1847 Ulverscroft Priory purchased by Henry Grey 7th Earl of Stamford.
1847 Bradgate plantations: Sliding Stone, Elder Tree & Holgate Hill in Bradgate (16acres) begun.
1850 William Martin Bradgate estate manager dies.
1851 Population: Post Office Directory, Cropston 112 persons, Groby 441 persons and Newtown Linford 483 persons.
1854/55 Many outbreaks of cholera in England.
1868 Cropston reservoir wall (within park on north side) built by George Rudkin of Groby – 1300 yards.
1883 George - Harry, Earl of Stamford dies. His cousin the Rev Harry Grey becomes 8th Earl of Stamford.
1886 Slate quarries at Groby and Swithland close.
1888 Groby slate quarry reopened by Charles Wesley.
1890 Rev Harry, 8th Earl of Stamford dies. His Nephew, William, becomes 9th Earl of Stamford.

A time line...Events

1902	Groby Granite Quarry. Numbers of men from surrounding villages shown on pay roll at this time:-

Kirby Muxloe	13
Markfield	16
Anstey	34
Newtown Linford	58
Glenfield	66
Ratby	173
Groby	186

1908	Groby slate quarry (the last working slate quarry in Leicestershire) closes as Charles Wesley gives up lease.
1910	The 9th Earl of Stamford dies and Roger, the last Earl of Stamford, becomes the 10th Earl.
1921	Ulverscroft Priory sold to T.P. Towle Esq. of Loughborough by Mrs. Grey.
1925	Bradgate Estate sold.
1927	Ulverscroft Priory purchased by W. Linsay Everard Esq. of Ratcliffe Hall.
1941	At least six small 'Tea Rooms' as well as other cottages selling jugs of tea in Newtown Linford, the village is busy with summer visitors.
1941	Upwards of one hundred soldiers living under canvas in Bradgate Park. Home Guard Commando company formed in Leicester also trains in Bradgate Park. Map reading and gunnery exercises carried out there. Bren gun carriers also used within park.
1943	A.T.S. wireless operators from Beaumanor in huts behind Bradgate Arms and village hall, Newtown Linford.
1945	Dunlop Rubber Company stops finishing of parts in Newtown Linford British Legion Club 7th May 1945.
1946	Newtown Linford has company of ATS girls, attached to R.A.O.C. stationed in Church Hall and immediately to rear of Bradgate Arms Hotel. They march daily to the Methodist Church Rooms, Anstey for their breakfast before reporting for work at a tank refurbishment depot located on the New Parks Estate, Leicester.
1976	The 10th Earl of Stamford dies and the male Grey family line becomes extinct.

A time line...Events

1976   Dunham Massey becomes a National Trust property, as a gift, on the death of Roger Grey, 10th Earl of Stamford.

References
The Population of England 1541 – 1871 (a reconstruction)

E.A. Wrigley and R.S.Schofield, published by Edward Arnold. 1983 at £45.00, indicates the health crisis years as 1542/3, 1557/58, 1563/4, 1590/91, 1597, 1603, 1609/10, 1613/14, 1625, 1639/10, 1665, 1670/71, 1678/79/80/81/82/83/84/85 1729, 1742/43 1766/67, 1779/80/81/82/83/84 1802, 1854/55
The assumption that the above are likely plague years is based on the higher than average number of deaths during these years.

The Transformation of Medieval England 1370 - 1529
John A.F. Thomson, Longman 1983 in paperback.
ISBN 0 - 582 - 48975 - X

Visitations of the Plague at Leicester, William Kelly. F. R.H.S. 1877.

In the case of major epidemics, it is often impossible to specify the precise disease as contemporary records are often imprecise.
The term 'plague' may denote an epidemic of bubonic or pneumonic plague, but it may also be used more generally to describe any pestilence. How widespread epidemics were is impossible to say and the nature of the disease 'sweating sickness' – see 1551 Darley Dale – is far from clear.

In addition to dates given above, which were derived from national registers, the epidemics within Derbyshire and Leicestershire have been noted wherever the information shows a lengthening of the periods already noted, or crisis years peculiar to this area.

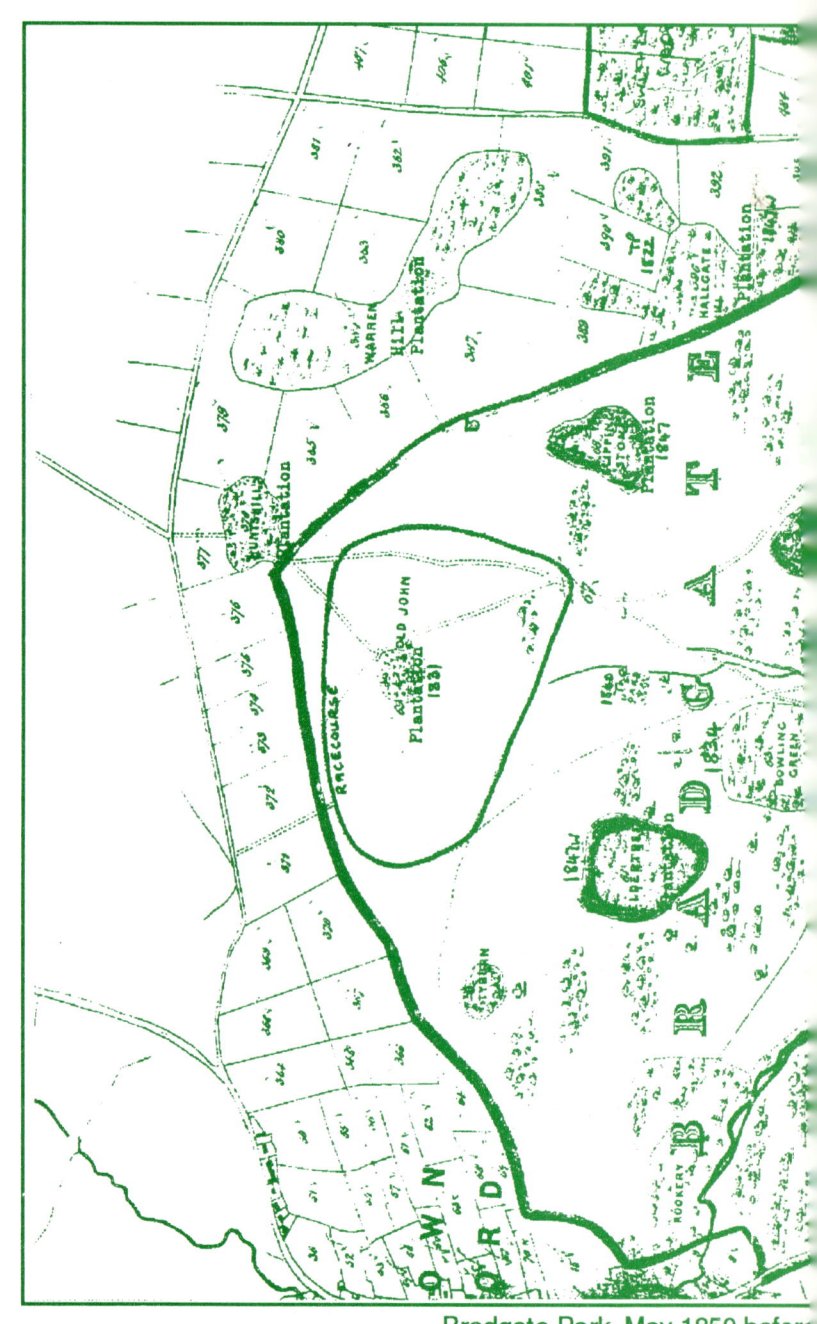

Bradgate Park, May 1859 before

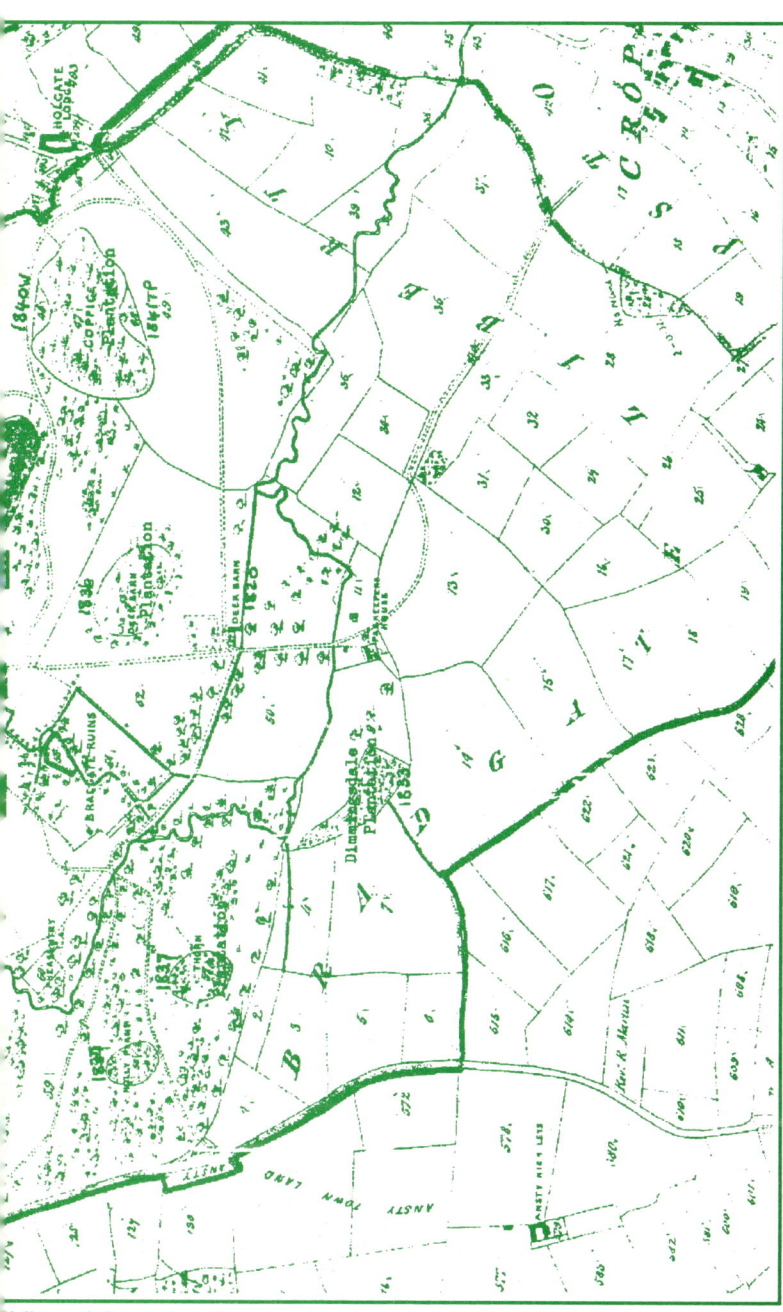

ilding of Cropston Reservoir

OLD JOHN
Fact or Fiction?

Few counties can lay claim to such a well known folly as the tower on John Hill in Bradgate Park, Leicestershire and the myths and legends associated with this tower certainly far exceed the realms of credibility at times!

John Hill in the north-western corner of Bradgate Park was originally the site of a windmill of the 'post' type until the summer of 1784. During the violent summer of that year the mill was either blown down in the severe storms which swept Britain and parts of Europe throughout June, July and August, or it became so unsafe that it was taken down and in its place was built the familiar tower which we know so well today. None of the original windmill was incorporated in the new building as the former was an all wooden construction frequently serviced by carpenters from Newtown Linford.

The mason responsible for building the tower, Thomas Sketchley of Anstey, had been employed by the Earl of Stamford, mainly on bridge and wall building on the Bradgate Estate for some forty years previously. There is a theory which lies well within the bounds of credibility that John Hope, a Cheshire architect who designed the folly built at Mow Cop, Cheshire in 1754 may well have produced the design for the Bradgate Tower. As John Hope also worked for the Earl of Stamford on his Enville Estate in Staffordshire this theory would appear to have some substance. For as well as the size and shape of the towers and their appendage arches, even arched headed windows in Gothic Revival style feature on both follies.

The building of the tower on John Hill coincided with the cutting back of Charnwood Forest from Newtown Linford village to Hunts Hill, at the north-western end of Bradgate Park. The clearance of this area enabled William Platts, the miller who had previously held both the watermill, near Bradgate House and the windmill on John Hill to erect another windmill in 1789 on the newly disaforrested ground on Lint Hill in Newtown. (William Platts had by this time

Old John

taken a lease on Lint Hill Farm at the foot of Lint Hill towards Sharpley Hill.) Due to this windmill's short life and very low rental payments of six pence per year it may well be that Platts was allowed to transport the remains of the old post mill to the newly cleared Lint Hill site.

Close by Ulverscroft watermill had been built and was working by 1800 with William Platts' eldest son, Thomas Platts in charge. The Lint Hill mill can be traced through rent book entries to this same date of 1800 but not beyond. William Platts' windmill was it seems a short lived venture assuming of course that it ever reached working condition.

(The Platts family can be traced as millers living at the Groby watermill, close to Groby Pool in 1762-1764. William father of the above William Platts being in charge at this earlier time.)

Mow Cop (on the Cheshire/Staffordshire border) was built in 1754.
This became the model for Old John but the Earl of Stamford rejected the roundels for the more usual lancet windows.

Old John

The folly at Mow Cop, Cheshire, which bears a striking similarity to the tower at Bradgate was built as an open ruin and remains so even today. The tower on John Hill, referred to locally as 'Old John', would appear to have been built with hunting, racing time trials and shelter in mind, for an upper floor giving superb views over the Park can be reached via a staircase inside the tower. Slate fireplaces contemporary with the tower building date can be found on both the ground and first floors. The above begs the question, was the Bradgate tower originally built as an open ruin?

Malcolm's illustration for John Nichols, *The History and Antiquities of the County of Leicester* shows a tower without crenellations or windows in the etching dated 1792. Sketchley is known to have returned to carry out work on the tower after its building and it may well be that the mock ruin was altered shortly after the original building date of October 1784.

Nowadays the shallow crenellations on top of the tower can be reached from within the upper floor but with no proper support behind them they are just a decorative feature. Observations on horses being trained on a course which ran around the tower were perhaps meant to be made from inside the building, the best vantage points being from the first floor windows; the small walled plantation (c.1832) growing close to the tower was not at this early date obscuring the all round view of the circular racecourse.

It is certainly true that the archway attached to the tower on the stable, or south side of the tower was considerably longer in earlier days. A sketch made by John Flower in the mid nineteenth century shows the appendage archway, plus mock rustic walling stretching at least four times the length of the present day archway. The additional walling in Flower's sketch contains three lancet arches at various heights above ground. Late nineteenth century post cards of the tower

Old John

record that the 'handle' feature was at least twice the length of the existing archway and the break point has shortened the arch to bisect the second lancet window. Thus making the legend of the old retainer's death being marked by a monument built like a beer tankard of recent origin.

Sketch drawn by John Flower (1793-1861)

Old John

Another of the tales told about the tower is that it is named after 'Old John' a miller who was killed at the bonfire held on 'John Hill' in celebration of The Earl of Stamford's son's coming of age. 'Old John' was, according to the legend, struck and killed by a burning pole falling from the fire in these celebrations of 1786. There are however a number of facts which fail to support this story. 'John Hill' on which the tower stands is featured on a map of the park dated 1746. Therefore the name given to both the hill and that of the tower can be established before the 'death' of the miller it is supposedly named after. Further, the tower was built by Thomas Sketchley, an Anstey mason in 1784 and his payments for the work are recorded in the Bradgate Estate accounts in the autumn of that year, two years before the supposed dedication to the unfortunate miller.

The Earl of Stamford's son, later the 6th Earl of Stamford, reached the age of twenty one in 1786 and celebrations including the lighting of a bonfire on John Hill can be verified through newspaper reports of the event, but it is with equal certainty that no miller by the name of John worked the Bradgate Park mills during the 18th century. John Allman of Groby mill is seemingly the only estate miller called John who just might fit the legend. He had retired to a cottage on the Ratby Waste by 1779 and this name can be traced through the estate papers after this date until 1808. It is of course possible that John Allman senior had a son named after him and John junior continued to live in the Ratby cottage so this is perhaps not a sound line of enquiry to follow. However after such a tragic accident the unfortunate 'John' would have been buried in Newtown Linford churchyard where many of the faithful servants to the Earl of Stamford lie at rest. No stone there records John's unfortunate passing in 1786 and the burial register also remains strangely silent, as do the church registers of other villages close to Bradgate

Mills on Bradgate Estate

There were two 'Bradgate' mills, one windmill on Old John hill and a watermill to the east of the chapel c.1500-1784.

BRADGATE MILLS

1540	Thomas Poultney (Knight)	
1633	Richard Broadhurst age 68 dies	
1636	William Gulson	
1670	Robert Wheatley	(marriage register)
1738	Thomas Platts	per year £8 0 0
1739	Thomas Page	per year £8 0 0
1740	Thomas Page	per year £8 0 0
		arrears £4 0 0
1748	David Warner	the mills
1774	David Warner	£6 0 0
1782	David Warner	£6 0 0
1783	WIlliam Platts	£6 0 0
1785	William Platts moves to farm	
	Bradgate mills not mentioned after this date	
1789	William Platts windmill on the Lint Hill (Newtown) 6d	
1790	William Platts windmill on the Lint Hill (Newtown) 6d	
1800	William Platts windmill on the Lint Hill (Newtown) 6d	

The old watermill, BradgatePark c.1841

Mills on Bradgate Estate

ANSTEY MILL
(water course payment only – the miller is likely to be a different person).

1656	John Corbett	1d
1677	Robert Bradfield	1d
1738	Richard Bradfield	1d
1792	Thomas Griffin	1d
1792	Thomas Griffin	1d
1800	Thomas Griffin	1d
1810	Thomas Griffin (Edward Hook ditto)	1d
1815	Thomas Platt (late Griffin)	1d
1825	Thomas Platt	1d
1828	Thomas Pares Esq. (late Platt)	1d
1850	Thomas Pares Esq.	1d
1877	Shirley Wain	1d
1904	Shirley Wain	1d

Mills on Bradgate Estate

Lint Hill Farm, Newtown Linford.
The former 'Bucks Head' photographed May 1988

This was the home of the Matts family between 1784 and 1850. William Matts was the last miller to lease both the wind and water mills in Bradgate Park.

William took over the Ulverscroft mill in 1800 and also developed the Lint Hill Farm buildings into a successful inn called the 'Bucks Head'.

Local tradition has it that stage coaches stopped here. As the Earl of Stamford's Bradgate Steward is known to have used the Birmingham to Leicester coach to convey messages and game to the Earl at Enville Hall, near Kidderminster, during the 1830s there may be some substance in this tale.

Mills on Bradgate Estate

ULVERSCROFT MILL

1745	George Abell (early mill – site/new 1800 mill)
1800	Thomas Platts (new mill)
1849	Thomas Platts
1851	Thomas Wesley – mill shown as late Cunningham (?)
1859	Henry King(?)

Ulverscroft Mill in 1988 – given a new roof 1993
Built originally with 3 storeys, 2 pairs of stones, wash house, trap house, coach place, stable, poultry place, mixing house, pig house.

Mills on Bradgate Estate

GLENFIELD MILLS

1664	????	Pooles
1650		Christopher Wright Clarke, one watermill late Pooles
1677		Christopker Wright Clarke
1825	W	Grant
1846	W	Green
1855Dr	T	Cufflin
1841	W	Hassall
1864	W	Hassall
1877	J.H.	Halford
1881	A	Ludlam
1899	A	Ludlam

THURMASTON MILLS – also part of Bradgate Estate

1669	Richard	Coates	hold watermill at full yearly value	£25 0s
1710	Hugh	Coates		
1738	John	Needham the mills		
1740	John	Needham the mills		
1758	Widow	Needham the mills	per year £14 10s	
1759	Widow	Needham the mills		
1763	Albine	Worsdale?		
1773	T	Worsdale		
1774	Daniel	Bishop		
1794	Edward	Bishop	watermill	
1823	Edward	Bishop	water and windmills	
1839	Edward	Bishop	watermill	
1839	Mr	Parr	land where mill stood	5s 0d
1840	Daniel	Bishop	watermill	
1840	Mr	Parr	land where mill stood	
1850	Daniel	Bishop		£10 0s
1850	William	Simkin	land where mill stood	5s 0d
1857	Daniel	Bishop		£10 0s
1877	Sarah	Gibbons	millers and bakers	
1881	Sarah	Gibbons & Son millers and bakers		

Mills on Bradgate Estate

GROBY MILLS

1540	Randolf	Fox
1572	Anthony	Sackford — two watermills
1636	Windmill mentioned on Fletcher land near Kitebridge	
1647	Wlliam	Roulson (also Roleson) two watermills and one windmill
1658	William	Roulson (March) — two watermills
1658	Richard	Hobson – Poole Mills
1669	William	Roulson
1677	Richard	Hobson holds two mills £16 0s
1698	Thomas	Gunley
1724	Thomas	Gumley (dies)
1736	Thomas	Ingram in arrears for mills and lands
1737	Thomas	Everit £16 10s
1738?	John	Hopkinson
1740?	John	Hopkinson (died 1741)
1744	John	Allman
1758	John	Allman
1759	John	Allman/Francis Smith
1762	William	Platts of Newtwon Linford
1764	William	Platts
1765	Reuben	Stevenson of Measham £20 0s
1800	Reuben	Stevenson mill and land ½ year = £13 7s
1808	Thomas	Cufflin, house, mill and land – part Barn Hills £13 7s
1835	Thomas	Cufflin, house, mill and land – part Barn Hills £13 7s
1836	Francis	Doleman and John Stokes, house, mill and land £20 5s
1840	Francis	Doleman, house, mill and land £16 15s
1850	Joseph	Thomson, windmill and land – plot 80
1857	Thomas	Wesley of Newtown, watermill and land – plot 120
1864	George	Aspell "at the timber yard of Groby Mill".
1870	George	Aspell "at the timber yard of Groby Mill".

The Tower and its Connection with Horse Racing

The tower's connection with horse racing can be partly established through original estate papers and with developments connected with fox hunting. As the pace of the hunt followers increased the 5th Earl of Stamford, George - Harry and later his brother, the Hon. Booth Grey, appear to have become very keen both on hunting and horse racing.

Numerous developments in the breeding of all animals were taking place in the latter half of the 18th century. Robert Bakewell's selective breeding methods witnessed by scores of visitors to Dishley Grange, near Loughborough were obvious to all, and what could be achieved with cattle, sheep and the old English heavy horse could equally well be applied to the type of horse and hound required for hunting. The history of hunting and horse racing up until this period makes interesting and necessary background reading to understand what was happening in Bradgate Park during the 18th century.

The majority of horse races prior to 1780 were for mature animals over at least two miles and in north east Leicestershire there are records in newspapers of ten mile races well after this date. At the same time however there was a growing tendency, particularly in the north of England, to race younger horses, encouraging the development of speed by matching them over shorter distances. The Oaks, a race for three year old fillies and run over one and a half miles was established at the Epsom meeting in May 1778. The experiment proved a success and a new race for both colts and fillies to be run over one mile was arranged for 4th May 1780. The prize was £1,065.15s.0d. The Grey family are known to have been racing horses at this time but it was not until 1812 when Lord Stamford's brother, Mr Booth Grey had a colt which ran unplaced in the Derby that the family name makes an appearance with horses of very high quality. From the Grey family Leicestershire estate records it can be seen that a new eleven stall stable had been erected in Bradgate Park

Old John and horse racing

by Thomas Cramp, a carpenter from Ratby during June/August 1781. So it would appear that the training of horses within the park was already established by this time.

Throsby writes in his, *Select Views in Leicestershire* 1789, that hounds and horses were kept near the Bradgate House ruins at this time. Mr Booth Grey used part of the estate steward's (William Mason) house at Stewards 'Hay, Groby as a hunting seat when visiting Leicestershire One of the largest payments received for keeping horses in the park, £43.0.0, came from a Mr. Hardy in 1789 and again in 1790. Mr. Hardy and the Hon. Mr. Willoughby were later to race in a challenge race from Melton Mowbray to Dalby Wood for 1,000 guineas. *The Leicester Journal,* March 23rd 1792 reports that on Friday last a match of an extraordinary kind was run over the country, from Melton Mowbray to Dalby Wood (distance 10 miles) for 100 guineas a side between a horse belonging to Mr Hardy, got by the Rutland Arabian, rode by Mr. Loraine Smith's valet, against a capital hunter of the Hon Mr Willoughby's; rode by his whipper-in, which was won by the former by a distance of nearly two miles. The starting odds at starting were 6 and 7 to 4 against the latter, and in running 20 and 100 to 1 in favour of the Arabian.

Hunting matches were races behind hounds, these chasing a stag or a buck. The first recorded races of this type occur in the reign of James I (1603-1625). In Charles II's reign (1660-1685): "This day, for a wager before the king, my lords of Castlehaven, and Arran... did run down and kill stout buck in St James's Park". The earliest steeplechase matches were between hunters, their owners riding, crossing country from a start-point to some distant but visible objective. The first recorded match of this kind was held in Ireland in 1752 though there is also evidence that it was Leicestershire where this type of racing first started. Such matches were run slowly, because hunting was a more leisurely sport in those days.

Hounds in the mid 18th century were cross breeds but

Old John and horse racing

predominantly bloodhound, a heavy dog with an unhurried action. At the same time the old English Hunter was a strong half-bred horse somewhere between a racer and a light cart mare. In the 1750s and 1760s however hunting was to be transformed and the event which caused this transformation happened in 1763. A match had been arranged at Newmarket between the Cheshire hounds,- bred on the principle, of Mr Smith Barry – and the Quorn hounds, bred on the old principle, of Hugo Meynell. Smith Barry's hounds, following a drag, won by a great distance. All foxhounds thereafter became lighter, quieter and far faster due to a greyhound cross. To follow them, hunting men had to quickly acquire faster horses. By about 1770 all eminent hunts had their share of thoroughbred and part thoroughbred horses. The owners of these new swift running horses began to treat the hunting field as a place to race and subsequently numerous challenges were issued. The challenges normally took the form of match races, two horses raced for the most part in a straight line and usually over a distance of four miles. The riders usually followed a lead, this meant a third party going forward with a scent marking drag to the spot where the match was to end. In the late 18th century matches it was the norm to have a couple of hounds running at the same time.

The dogs were gradually phased out and by 1800 it was more normal for the contestants to follow a pilot horse ridden by a hunt servant who knew the country extremely well. Usually the pilot started some 60 yards (20 metres) ahead and by waving a handkerchief he would indicate where fences might be jumped. Mounted spectators, some quite openly pacing for one of the contestants, were a real hazard. It was a practice forbidden by the Jockey Club on established racecourses, yet still causing problems as late as 1838. There were numerous occasions when undisciplined crowds spoilt a race just as the leading horse was nearing the winning post. At Epsom, on the first day of the October meeting 1776, just as the leading horse approached the winning post he was crossed by an

Old John and horse racing

unknown rider on horseback, the race leader was thrown. Fortunately the horse carried the rider, with foot still hanging in stirrup, beyond the winning post, where it was deemed that the rider's weight had travelled the prescribed distance. The jockey miraculously had avoided injury. Epsom seems to have been unusually casual about how its meetings were conducted. One gentleman attending a meeting there in 1785 reported to friends after the event that, "horse racing and cock fighting are carried on there to the pitch of absolute madness. There are neither lists of runners nor barriers at these races. The horses run in the midst of the crowd, who leave only a space sufficient for them to pass through. At the same time the crowd will encourage the horses with loud shouts and gestures".

The way around the crowds and the other attendant difficulties when trying to safeguard the match riders, was to carry out the trials and matches where the public could be easily excluded. Bradgate Park offered a diversity of terrain within its confines and flat racing could be practised on the level ground close to the ruins of Bradgate House with jumps added by stacking bundles of kidds (bundles of cut fern) to simulate fences if these were required.

Secrecy could bring high dividends and it was still possible a half century after the first Derby in 1780 to enter a three year old horse in the race which had, 'done enough at home to suggest it might easily win in a moderate year'. The Derby winner Frederick in 1829 had never run on a recognised race course before – his starting odds were 40:1 against. Again in 1835 Mundig, a horse belonging to John Bowes of Strethlam Castle, County Durham and showing much promise, was entered for the Derby by the Duke of Cumberland, one of John Bowes's trustees. Bowes was only 21 and still at Cambridge. The odds secured, without Bowes knowing the horse had even been entered, were long. Bowes found out what was about to happen and called a meeting of his trustees. Failing to bluff their way through a tricky situation the trustees were forced to transfer the most

Old John and horse racing

favourable bets laid, over to John Bowes. Mundig won by a head and John Bowes collected £20,000 from the bet and £3,500 for winning the race. A year later after winning three races and losing three Mundig was retired to the stud at Market Harborough at a ten guinea fee.

To train horses away from the public eye very much appealed to Lord Stamford and a small group of other Leicestershire racehorse owning enthusiasts. From the above stories it can be seen that the rewards could be very high even if lesser races were to be the targets. It is unfortunate that the estate records are compiled in such away that only a yearly amount is cash is recorded for joisting (animals kept in the park at a fixed rent) but occasionally fuller details are given. In 1758 £10 7s 8d was collected from horse owners keeping horses in 'The Parks'. Sections within Bradgate are referred to as 'High Park' north of the central wall 'Low Park' south of the central wall or 'The Copy' an area close to Hallgates used for cattle at this time.

Sometimes more detailed notes are available as in 1828 when Mr Paget of Groby had one horse in training for seven weeks, Mr Grocock of Kilby had a horse in training for thirteen weeks, Mr Pratt of Leicester, Mrs Ward of Belgrave and Colonel Wolleston of Shenton all had one horse in training for ten weeks. Ten weeks incidentally was thought to be the length of time required to get a gross horse fit to race. The beauty of the screening methods adopted by Lord Stamford's friends was that once a likely horse was found for a particular event it could be moved close to Lord Stamford's Staffordshire House, Enville Hall, where a replica Epsom track had been built on a clearing within woodland well away from public roads. Success did not come cheaply however for apart from feeding, stabling and training horses, there was the added difficulty of moving horses from one meeting to another. Prior to 1816 when mention is made of a Mr Territt sending his horse Sovereign from Worcestershire to Newmarket in a bullock-cart all race horses were walked to race

Old John and horse racing

meetings. Given that a gentleman had a number of horses in training he might well need a very large staff just to move his horses around the country.

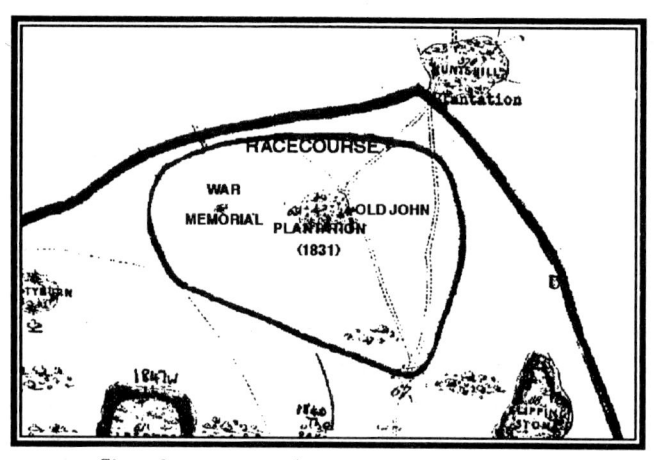

Site of racecourse (see map on pages 22/23)

It is not until the 7th Earl of Stamford's horse *Diophantus* won the 2,000 guineas in 1861 that the family appears to have enjoyed a little return for such a large investment in keeping a fine stable of horses. Even with well fancied horses there were great disappointments. In the 1862 Derby, Lord Stamford's Ensign at 25:1 was left at the start. Again in 1870 the horse *Normandy* at 33:1 was unplaced. In 1882 there was a small return on all money spent on the sport when *Geheimniss* won the Oaks. For the race *Geheimniss* had been trained at Kingsclere near Newbury, Berkshire and also in the same stable was that year's Derby winner *Shotover* belonging to the Duke of Westminster. Lord Stamford and the Duke of Westminster both celebrated their good fortune by holding a huge picnic on the neighbouring Downs. Everyone in the village was entertained and air balloons in the colours of both owners were released before fireworks rounded off the evening. The stones marking the

Old John and horse racing

Bradgate Park match race track lie hidden under ferns today. The distance around the oval circuit, ringing Old John tower being about a mile and a quarter. From the races won it would appear that success in the Derby, Oaks and the 2,000 guineas was sought for many years but although successful in the latter two races over long periods of time the Derby remained an elusive goal.

When Lord Stamford gave up the Quorn hunt in 1863 – he was master there from 1856 to 1863 – it is thought that upwards of 7,000 people attended the Tattersall's auction to see seventy-nine horses sell for 14,350 guineas, a clear indication of the running costs involved for a master of a top class hunt. What is perhaps less well-known, and overlooked by countless writers at the time and later, is that Lord Stamford had asked Joseph Dawson – regarded as one of the top thoroughbred racehorse trainers at that time to be his private trainer at Newmarket in 1861. The interests of Lord Stamford were changing for foxes were difficult to find and the fox count was reported as low. The Earl would buy foxes at Dunham Massey and move them to his own 9,000 acres of Leicestershire land. His desire to win the Derby seems to have taken a great deal of his attention away from the Quorn and hunting in general.

The money from Tattersall's sale of his hunters was immediately used to help increase Lord Stamford's stable of racing thoroughbreds. From the Racing Calendar it is possible to trace thirteen horses actually running at his favourite racecourses in 1863 – there were probably at least twenty to thirty horses in training at the time – and by 1865, eighteen horses are running under Lord Stamford's colours of light blue, black and gold belt, and black cap. After the Oaks win by *Geheimniss* in 1882 Lord Stamford may well have decided that enough was enough. His health was most decidedly failing – he was to die the following year – and by his own reckoning he had spent a quarter of a million pounds in pursuit of winning the Derby.

Old John and horse racing

Race course and horses connected with Lord Stamford (i)

1783 Leicester : Lord Stamford's bay horse 4th but no name given.

1790 Bridgnorth, Leicester, Lichfield, Warwick and Worcester
     Horse : Florizel.

1791 Burford, Chester, Grantham and Nottingham
     Horses : Caractacus, Florizel and Skylark.

1795 Bridgnorth, Hereford, Ludlow, Nantwich, Warwick and Worcester.
     Horses : Rudrough, a SYO and Tiger.
     Lord Grey : a SYO br c by Sir Peter Teazle.

1799 Leicester : Lord Stamford ch h George 6YO by Dungannon 1st.
     Bridgnorth, Derby, Knutsford, Lichfield, Ludlow, Newcastle-under-Lyme, Northampton, Nottingham, Warwick.
     Horses : Alfred, George, Petrina and Scotilla.

1801 Leicester : Lord Stamford's ch Chanter 4YO 1st

1803 Leicester : Lord Grey's horse: Edger a 5YO 1st, 2nd, 2nd.

1805 Leicester : Lord Stamford's br c : Gayman 4YO.

1808 Leicester : Mr. Grey's b.f. : Belinda 4YO.

1809 Leicester : Lord Stamford's horse : Gustavus.

1820 Chester : Astrolger, Comet, Magician, Rainbow and Tarquin.
     Knutsford : Astologer and Magician.
     Preston : Comet and Magician.
     Worcester : Comet and Rainbow.

1825 Knutsford : Horse Landrail 26.07.1825.

1835 Lord Stamford has no horse running.

1835 Lord Grey (Enville) deceased. Horses: Enville a 4YO, King Cole.
     Courses : Chester and Worcester.

1840 and 1850 no reference to Lord Stamford found.

1861 Newmarket : Malta 3YO winner of 50 sovereign plate.

1863 Newmarket : Aetna, Cerintha, Chicot, Citadel, Corsica, Diviner, Flying Fish, Good for Nothing, Lady Augusta, Onesander, Oscar, Revolve, Romanoff.

1864 Newmarket : Acolyte, Britannia, Cabuscan, Gemma, Gownsman, Hawks-Eye, Leicester, Revolver, Tourist, Venus.

Old John and horse racing

Race course and horses cont

1865	Bath and Somerset, Croxton Park (Leicestershire), Epsom, Newmarket, Northampton and Pytchley Hunt, Lincoln, Liverpool.		
	Warwick	:	Archimedes, Beizon, Brick, Cambuscan, Chibsa, Esca, Freedom, Guinea, Isabella, Queen Bee, Rejection, Spring Gun, Thalessiu, Venus, Willis Sharp, Zingal.
	Doncaster	:	St Ledger – Archimedes ran 3rd.
1870	Courses	:	Epsom, Newmarket, Warwick.
	Horses	:	Bradgate, 4YO, 3rd at Newmarket, Prince of Wales Stakes.
			Citadel, 2YO, 1st at Newmarket.
			My Lady, 3YO, u/p at Newmarket.
			Normanby, u/p at Epsom (Derby).
			Parmesan, 3YO, 1st at Newmarket.
			Pompeii, 4YO, 1st at Warwick.
1872/1875,1880,		No Oaks or Derby runners.	
1882	Horses	:	Geheimniss winns the Oaks at Epsom.
			Incognita 3YO u/p at Newmarket.
		I	Miniture 2YO u/p at Newmarket.
1885/1890			No Oaks or Derby runners.

Croxton Park, Leicestershire: first races in Racing Calendar 1826 latest noted in 1865 but this may not be the last. Races for half-bred hunters.

Old John and horse racing

Old John Tower viewed from horse stalls.
After racing around the tower the horses were rubbed down here and the horse owners met inside the tower.

Old John Tower was almost certainly first built as a mock open ruin, very similar to that which stands on a hillside called Mow Cop in Staffordshire. After the tower on John Hill reached completion in 1784 its builder Thomas Sketchley, of Anstey was asked to return on at least two occasions to modify previous work. It is during this period that the folly was floored, walled completely, glazed and roofed. Social friends were then able to view the horse trials in comfort – a small chimney and firegrates being added to the upper and lower floors. The spinney on John Hill was not added until 1832 and up to this time it was possible to watch the horses galloping around the greater part of the 'racing' circuit around the tower. Rubbing down stalls were to be added below the tower on the southern side of the hill at a much later date, necessitating the removal of a large portion of the appendage archway immediately above the stalls (c.1850). The familiar 'beer mug' shape of the tower upon John Hill is then of more recent date than the original stretched shape consisting of tower, arch and section of wall containing three lancet windows.

Old John and horse racing

Old John c. 1900
With appendage arch, one lancet window and horse stalls.
The roof timbers to stalls have lost their slates.

Old John Tower in the 1990s

Mow Cop and Old John

Mow Cop

There seems to be a very strong link between the follies of Mow Cop, on the Cheshire/Staffordshire border and Old John in Bradgate Park, Leicestershire. John Hope, a Cheshire architect designed the folly built at Mow Cop in 1754. Hope was also employed on various projects connected with Enville Hall in Staffordshire, one of three large houses belonging to the Earl of Stamford – the others being Bradgate House and Dunham Massey Hall, near Manchester. The link with John Hope would appear to have some substance for the similarity in design is quite marked if one remembers that Old John also had an extended ruined wing rather than just the present archway or 'handle' until late in the 19th century. The building date for Old John is September/October 1784 with additional work carried out shortly afterwards. There is a possibility that Old John was an open folly when first built by Thomas Sketchley, a mason from Anstey, for documents show he returned twice to do further building work at the tower before the year 1800.

Old John

Notes:

(a)   Henry 4th Earl of Stamford – b.1715, d.1768
George-Harry 5th Earl of Stamford – b.1737, d.1819
George-Harry 6th Earl of Stamford – b.1765, d.1845
George-Harry 7th Earl of Stamford – b.1827, d.1883

(b) Racing Calendar 1774-1890

(c) Newmarket public library collection of racing and hunting books.

An old postcard of Old John – date unknown

Butchers, Bakers & Candlestick makers

Trades in a Victorian street, Lutterworth, Leicestershire.

by

Lynda Hill and Roz Bailey

Who lived and worked in a typical Victorian street is portrayed here. Although this is Church Street in Lutterworth it could as easliy be any other market town during that period of our history.

For those who like to read about the reality, rather than the fiction, of those years – this book is a must.

ISBN No. 1 898884 07 2　　　　　　　**140pp　£5.25 (inc. p. & p.)**

Breakfast at Bradgate

Book 2 in the series of *Bradgate and its Villages* draws on some 170 shopping lists which is not normally anyone's idea of interesting reading material. However, if the contents of a book are based on shopping lists which are over 300 years old (1678-1681), it can be almost guaranteed that an initial curiosity will lead quite naturally to almost compulsive further reading.

Breakfast at Bradgate is not only an authentic record of what was eaten at Bradgate House during the reign of Charles II but is a true glimpse of daily life in the house and some of its many callers. The delivery boy who calls at the house with 26 lbs of butter, Mr. Burbridge who mends rabbit nets and Thomas Shaw who arrives with wire ready to ring the swine, are all carefully listed.

The variety and volume of food from local areas like the large numbers of woodcock taken within Bradgate Park towards Newtown, and the crayfish caught in dozens – on one occasion thirty-five dozen crayfish were taken in one week from the River Lyn – indicate a landscape which is host to sights and sounds almost unimaginable today. The rabbits, larks, fieldfares and blackbirds – remember four-and-twenty in a pie? – give a clear indication that all types of fresh meat were found locally.

If it was a fast day and guests were expected, then a fishing party would be sent to Groby Pool to take fresh carp, bream and pike. Distance appears to offer no major problems, Scarborough is mentioned as the place from where cod was purchased and a barrel of oysters and three lobsters are received from the east coast. Oranges and lemons are plentiful but coffee and tea were not items that appear on the Steward of the Kitchens weekly requisition.

The kitchen boys turn the spits as Anne Poole retires from her post and hands 24 pewter dishes over to her replacement in the scullery, Suzanna Carre. A tinker called to mend the lid in the kitchen water boiler, and a silver salver and five plates are packed in readiness to be sent to London.   *28th August 1681*

ISBN No. 1 898884 09 9   To be published 1996

V·O·L·C·A·N·O
PUBLISHING

For a list of all our publications
please write to
Volcano Publishing
13 Little Lunnon, Dunton Bassett, LE17 5JR